Tug of Words: Speak with Confidence and Truth
© 2025 by Rachel Closson. All rights reserved.

Published independently by Rachel Closson
rachelclosson.com

ISBN: 979-8-218-87599-2

Cover design and interior layout by Rachel Closson
Illustrations created using AI under the direction of the author

Printed in the United States of America.

First Edition
10 9 8 7 6 5 4 3 2 1

Created with love to help kids speak with confidence, courage, and truth.

DEDICATION

To my two beautiful children—

Being your mom is one of the greatest honors of my life.

You've stretched me, strengthened me, and made me want to become the woman God created me to be. Because of you, I've learned more about love, patience, and the kind of character God continues to shape within me.

Raising you has turned my heart both inward and upward. God has used you to teach me to slow down, to listen, and to lead with grace and courage.

And as He continues to grow me, I pray you'll allow Him to grow you too. More than anything, I want you to build your life on His truth. A steady, unshakable foundation that will guide you no matter how life shifts or changes.

Stand boldly for what's right, even when it's hard.
Love deeply, but with wisdom.
Lead with courage and carry humility with you always.

You can do anything when your confidence comes from who you are in Christ. And I hope you always know how proud I am of you, your honest hearts, your willingness to grow, and the way you rise again when life feels heavy.

When you walk in truth, speak with courage, and live with compassion, your life becomes a light in a broken world.

So keep shining.
Keep growing.
Keep choosing Him.

Because with God, you won't just make a difference— you'll change the world.

Love you both so much ♡ mom

PROLOGUE

Have you ever played tug-of-war?

Two teams pulling on the same rope—each one trying to win, muscles straining, faces red, feet digging into the ground. Nobody wants to let go first.

Words can feel the same way sometimes.
When we get upset, our words can turn into ropes.

We pull to prove a point.
We pull to feel heard.
We pull because if we stop, we might lose.

But the truth is, when words turn into a tug-of-war, nobody really wins. Even if one side "gets their way," everyone ends up tired, frustrated, or hurt.

What if we could play a different kind of game?
One where we drop the rope before anyone gets pulled down.
One where we listen, speak honestly, and still stay connected.

That's what this book is about.
Learning how to pause, breathe, and choose differently— so our words can build bridges instead of battles.

The strongest people aren't the ones who pull the hardest.
They're the ones who know when to stop pulling —
and start understanding.

INTRODUCTION

At the time of writing, my children are seven and fifteen. My own journey of self-awareness and growth has been unfolding for years, and once you begin to see things differently, you can't unsee them.

I kept thinking, If I am continuing to lean into the woman God created me to be, I want to help my kids—and someday their kids—grow into who He created them to be too. More than anything, I want them to remember that Jesus is the source of truth, the giver of life, and the only place real freedom is found.

> *Jesus said, "You will know the truth, and the truth will set you free"* (John 8:32).
> That freedom grows as we walk with Him and learn to live from who He says we are.

God invites all of us to live truthfully with honesty, courage, compassion, and grace. And I want my children to carry that truth in their hearts. Not just that they have a voice, but that *they are loved, seen, and called by God Himself.* Their worth doesn't come from approval, performance, or perfection. It comes from Him.

Because when we spend our lives chasing acceptance, we lose the *authenticity* God designed us to carry.

This book is about that journey.

It's about healthy communication, real connection, community, and honoring truth in the small, everyday moments that shape who we become.

And it's about remembering who you are—even in the middle of big emotions, hard choices, and growing-up lessons.

That's why I wrote **Tug of Words.**

HOW TO USE THIS BOOK — AND HOW IT WILL HELP

One chapter at a time
- Each chapter begins with a story, then moves into a truth, a moment to practice, and an activity. Let your child sit with each step before moving on. There's no rush—growth happens in small, honest moments.

Practice it out loud
- Kids learn best by doing. Encourage them to speak the brave words, role-play together, and even use a mirror to practice tone and confidence. Keep it lighthearted—because standing in truth isn't meant to feel heavy or like a chore.

Make it personal
- The prompts and activities are spaces for kids to write, draw, and imagine how they'd use brave words in their own life. Let their creativity lead the way—and notice what truths come alive in their words.

Come back to it
- This isn't a one-time read. Keep it nearby and revisit chapters—before a new school year, during a tough friendship, or anytime your child needs a reminder that they have a choice in how they show up and speak truth.

This book is written for kids in elementary school—but the principles inside aren't just for kids. They're for everyone—young or old.

Because learning how to pause, choose differently, and speak with confidence and truth is something we never outgrow.

While this book is designed for kids to read and practice, it's also for the parents, teachers, and mentors who walk alongside them. You may find that the lessons here reshape your own conversations, too.

What You'll Discover Inside

Kids will learn how to:
- Recognize when words start to feel like a tug-of-war
- Pause, breathe, and choose brave words instead of louder ones
- Use simple, real-life scripts to solve problems with friends, siblings, and family

Parents and teachers will discover tools to guide kids through real-life conflicts—on the playground, in the classroom, and at home.

And through it all, kids will be reminded of this simple truth:

You don't have to be a "good kid." You get to choose differently—and that's what makes you strong!

TABLE of CONTENTS

Dedication
Prologue
Introduction
How to Use This Book — and How It Will Help

Closing
    Bonus Chapter: The Conversation That Closes the Gap
Certificate
Parent & Teacher Notes
About the Author

PART ONE
The Game of Arguments

How to handle disagreements without losing connection.

Arguments can feel like a game—two sides pulling, pushing, shouting—each one trying to win. It can start small.

Who gets the last cookie.
Whose turn it is.
Who's "right."

But before you know it, it's like a tug-of-war you never meant to join. The rope tightens, voices rise, and suddenly, it's not even about the cookie anymore— it's about being heard.

Here's the truth: most of the time, nobody really wins. You just end up louder, more frustrated, saying things you don't mean, and further apart from the person you care about.

That's why we're starting here.
Because before you can use Brave Words, you have to understand the game—how it starts, why it pulls you in, and what it takes to step out of it.

And here's the best part: you don't have to play it like everyone else. You can choose a new way—one that builds peace instead of pressure, connection instead of chaos, and strength instead of noise.

Now, let's step inside the game together and see where the arguments begin.

CHAPTER ONE
The Fight for the Ball

The playground buzzed with noise—kids running, laughing, jump ropes snapping on the blacktop. But right in the middle of the field, the noise suddenly stopped.

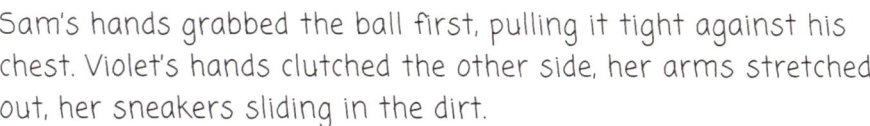

Violet and Sam were sprinting hard, eyes locked on the same basketball rolling to the grass.

Their arms pumped, feet pounding, both determined to reach it first. They collided in the middle.

Sam's hands grabbed the ball first, pulling it tight against his chest. Violet's hands clutched the other side, her arms stretched out, her sneakers sliding in the dirt.

"I had it first!" Sam shouted, his voice cracking.
"No, I did!" Violet yelled back, tugging harder.

Their sneakers scraped against the ground as they pulled in opposite directions. The ball wobbled between them, squeaking under the strain.

All around them, kids stopped what they were doing. The jump ropes stilled. The soccer game paused. Eyes turned. Whispers started. A few kids cheered, "Come on, Sam, don't let go!" Others shouted, "Violet's got this!"

And just like that, the game turned into a contest—an audience waiting to see who would win.

Sam's heartbeat thudded in his ears. His chest felt tight, the ball heavier in his hands. He wasn't just holding a ball—he was holding his pride. If I let go now, everyone will think I'm weak, he thought.

Violet's stomach twisted. Her arms ached, her fingers burning from gripping so tight. If I give up, everyone will think I'm a pushover, she told herself. She leaned back even harder, her jaw clenched, her face hot with frustration.

The longer they pulled, the less the ball even mattered. It wasn't about playing anymore—it was about winning. Sweat on Sam's forehead. Violet's breathing turned sharp and fast. The teacher's whistle blew from across the field, but neither one heard it.

They were too locked in, too focused on being right.
Around them, the laughter faded into an awkward hush.
The basketball squeaked again, caught in the middle of their tug-of-war—something meant for fun, now turned into a battle.

And here's the truth: The harder they pulled, the less fun anyone had. The louder they yelled, the less anyone listened.

By the time recess ended, nobody even remembered who had it first. They only remembered the fight. When the bell rang, kids scattered toward the door. The ball rolled away, a smudge of dirt across its side.

Sam kicked at the ground, his throat still tight. Violet walked off, blinking fast so no one would see her eyes shine.

Nobody said sorry. Nobody felt better. Just quiet footsteps and the echo of something that didn't have to happen.

The Tug-of-War Truth

Arguments are a lot like a game of tug-of-war. At first, it feels exciting—you grab hold and pull with all your strength.

You think, If I just pull harder, I'll win. But the longer you pull, the heavier it gets. Your arms ache. Your voice rises. Your heart feels tight. And even if you win, what do you really win? A dirty ball? A hurt friend?

That's what happened to Sam and Violet. They weren't just pulling on a ball—they were pulling on pride. Each wanted to be right more than they wanted to be kind.

Here's the truth:
Winning doesn't always mean you're strong.
Sometimes the strongest thing you can do is take a breath, loosen your grip, and choose peace over proving a point.

Brave words sound like this:
"Let's start over."
"You can go first."
"It's okay—we can share."

Because real courage isn't about shouting louder or holding tighter— it's about keeping your calm and **protecting** the friendship instead of the fight.

BRAVE WORDS IN ACTION

What if Sam had taken a deep breath
instead of pulling harder?

What if Violet had loosened her hands
instead of shouting louder?

The game could've ended with laughter instead of tears.
Different words can change the ending of any story.

Try these out loud:
"Let's take turns."
"It's not that big of a deal."
"We can play together."

Now imagine a rope stretched between my way and their way.
Right in the middle — that's where brave words live.

Pause for a moment and ask yourself:
"Which side am I pulling on today?"

Then whisper, "I can choose the middle."
Because every time you choose calm over chaos, you make space
for something stronger than winning— you make space for peace.

TEACHING FROM JESUS:

When you feel the pull to fight for what's yours, pause and look at the heart of the moment. Sometimes the strongest person isn't the one who wins the tug, but the one who lets go first. When you choose peace, you don't lose—you show love. I want you to be a peacemaker, because every time you choose calm instead of chaos, you *look more like Me.*

"Blessed are the peacemakers, for they will be called children of God."
— Matthew 5:9

Words That Grow With You

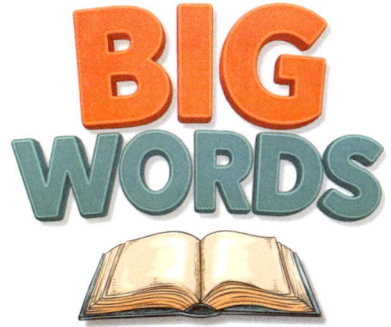

Clutched: *Held onto something very tightly.*
Sam clutched the ball against his chest, refusing to let go.

Strained: *Worked really hard until your muscles or body started to hurt.*
Violet strained as she pulled on the ball, her arms shaking with effort.

Defeated: *Feeling like you've lost or can't win anymore.*
When the teacher blew the whistle, both kids looked defeated, even though no one really won.

Responsibility: *Doing the right thing, even when it's hard.*
Sam learned that taking responsibility for his choices matters more than winning the ball.

When we choose peace over pride, everyone wins.

CHAPTER TWO
The Reading Corner

The classroom buzzed with excitement. It was story time—the part of the day everyone looked forward to.

Ms. Carter held up a brand-new book, the cover shiny and colorful. "All right, everyone," she said with a smile, "find your spot on the rug!"

Instantly, chairs scraped, shoes shuffled, and voices mixed with laughter as kids hurried toward the big oval carpet at the front of the room.

Lila darted forward, eyes locked on the sunny corner by the window. That was her favorite spot—the softest patch of the rug, with sunlight spilling across it like a warm blanket. She plopped down, hugged her knees, and smiled.

But just as she settled in, Jonah appeared. "Hey, that's my spot," he said, hands on his hips. "No, I was here first," Lila shot back, scooting an inch closer to the window.

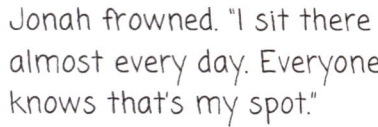

Jonah frowned. "I sit there almost every day. Everyone knows that's my spot."

Lila's cheeks burned. She pulled her knees in tighter. "Not today. I got here first."

The two glared at each other as a hush rippled through the room..

A few kids whispered. Some rolled their eyes. Others leaned closer, waiting to see who would win.

Jonah dropped his sweatshirt next to Lila like a tiny flag. "Move."
"No!" Lila's voice came out sharper than she meant.

The room grew quiet.

Ms. Carter raised an eyebrow but didn't step in right away. She
wanted to see if they could figure it out on their own.
But neither moved. Neither gave in.

What had started as story time had turned into a silent
standoff.

Finally, Ms. Carter sighed. "Jonah, just grab another spot so we
can get started," she said gently.

Jonah stomped to the other side of the rug, plopping down with a
heavy huff. His arms crossed, his face scrunched tight.

Lila stayed in her sunny spot—but
her chest felt heavy.

Here's the thing: neither one really
felt like they'd won.

Ms. Carter began to read the story,
but Jonah didn't hear a word. His mind was stuck on losing his
spot.

And Lila didn't feel happy either. Her sunny corner didn't feel so
warm anymore.

By holding onto the fight, they weren't just sitting on the rug.
They were carrying something heavier—like a backpack full of
bricks.

The Heavy Backpack

Arguments don't always look like yelling. Sometimes, they sound like silence that lasts too long. Sometimes, they feel like a heavy backpack full of bricks that you can't put down.

That's what Lila and Jonah carried. Even though the fight over the reading rug ended, neither one really felt okay.

Jonah's chest tightened, and Lila's shoulders sank as she stared at her shoes. No one said sorry, but both walked away heavier than before.

When we hold onto anger, it doesn't disappear — it just hides inside us. We replay the moment in our heads, we tell ourselves stories like "They were wrong," or "It's not fair."

And each thought adds another "brick" to that backpack.

But here's the truth: You can't climb higher while carrying extra weight. You can't move forward when you're still dragging yesterday behind you.

Sometimes, the bravest thing you can do is take off the backpack.

It starts with brave words like:
"I don't want to stay mad anymore."
"Let's start over."
"I forgive you."

Because brave kids don't wait for someone else to make it right. They choose to set down what's heavy and **walk lighter**.

BRAVE WORDS IN ACTION

What if Lila had looked up first?
What if she had said, "Jonah, maybe we can take turns."
or "We can both sit by the window next time."

The rug wouldn't have felt so crowded. Their hearts wouldn't have felt so heavy. Because sometimes, trying to win just makes everyone lose.

The truth is— you don't need to keep pulling to prove you're right.
You can pause, breathe, and choose kinder words.
That's what brave kids do.

They don't wait for someone else to fix it. They go first in kindness.

Different words lead to different endings. Instead of angry faces, you get smiles. Instead of silence, you get space to play together again.

Now it's your turn. Close your eyes and think of a time when you got mad about something small— like a turn, a toy, or a seat next to a friend.

Now take a slow breath and say:
"It's okay."
"I can try again."
"We can fix this together."

That's how brave kids help make things right. Not by pulling harder— but by choosing words that bring peace.

TEACHING FROM JESUS:

It's easy to hold tight to what feels fair. Kindness means stepping back so peace can grow. When your heart feels heavy after a fight, that's Me reminding you—being right will never matter more than being kind. Forgive quickly, love gently, and let your heart rest. You never lose when you choose *grace*.

Be kind and compassionate to one another, forgiving each other, just as in Christ God forgave you."
— Ephesians 4:32

Words That Grow With You

Darted: *Moved really fast, like a quick dash.*
Lila darted across the room to get the sunny corner of the reading rug.

Glared: *Stared at someone with an angry or mean look.*
Jonah glared at Lila, hoping she would move out of "his" spot.

Whispered: *Spoke in a very soft voice so only a few people could hear.*
The kids whispered to each other, waiting to see who would win the spot.

Heavy: *Describes something that weighs a lot or feels hard to carry — even feelings can feel heavy.*
Lila's chest felt heavy even though she'd "won" the spot on the rug.

When we choose kindness, everyone's story shines a little brighter.

CHAPTER THREE

The TV Remote Battle

The living room was supposed to be quiet, but it wasn't. The TV flickered, paused on the home screen. Sophia clutched the remote tight against her chest. James leaned over the couch, reaching for it.

> "I get to pick tonight!" Sophia shouted, her voice sharp.
> "No way!" James barked back. "It's my turn. You picked yesterday!"
> "That's not true!" Sophia's cheeks flushed. "You're just making that up!"

The bickering bounced back and forth between them, each word louder than the last. The dog barked. The show they both wanted to watch sat frozen on the screen, waiting.

> "Give it to me!" James lunged forward, his hand swiping at the remote.
> "No!" Sophia jerked it back, gripping harder. Her voice rose even higher—almost a scream.

The noise filled the room, bouncing off the walls. Their mom peeked her head in from the kitchen. "You both need to stop yelling and start communicating with a different tone, please. Yelling doesn't get anyone any further."

But her words seemed to just disappear between them. Sophia's shout was loud and furious. James shouted louder to drown her out. It was like a battle of volume instead of a battle of tug-of-war.

Then— **CRACK!**

Sophia had jumped up off the couch in frustration. The TV remote slipped from her hands, clattering to the floor. Batteries rolled out across the carpet.

"See what you did?" James snapped. "You broke it!"

"I didn't break it!" Sophia shot back. "This is your fault! If you would've just let me watch my show in the first place, we wouldn't be having this problem!"

James threw up his hands. "Here we go again—always blaming it on me!"

Their mom stepped in fully now, her voice calm but firm. "Pause." The room went quiet. Both kids froze, red-faced and fuming.

"Look," she said, pointing at the remote on the floor. "The louder your voices grew, the less anyone was actually listening. You weren't solving the problem—you were just making noise and pointing blame."

And there it was: the show still paused, the remote lying broken open, and no one happy.

Because when voices get loud, the words don't matter anymore. It's like turning up the music so high you can't even hear the song.

So next time you start to raise your voice, remember this: Is it about communicating louder? Or about communicating calmly and clearly?

Turned Up Too High

When voices get loud, something happens. The words stop being words. They turn into noise.

That's what Sophia and James forgot. Both wanted to be heard, but they kept turning up the volume until no one could understand anything anymore.

It's like when music gets too loud in the car. At first, it's fun. Then your ears start to hurt, and you can't even hear the song. That's what arguing does— it drowns out what really matters.

Yelling doesn't make your point stronger. It just makes the other person want to yell back. And then everyone feels upset, and nothing gets solved.

Here's what brave kids learn:
You can turn the volume down.
You can use calm words instead of loud ones.
You can take a deep breath, soften your voice,
and speak in a way that people want to listen.

Brave words sound like this:
"Let's talk, not yell."
"I'll go first, then you can share."
"Can we start over?"

Those words might feel small, but they're powerful. **They don't just fix the fight— they fix the feeling underneath it.**

BRAVE WORDS IN ACTION

What if Sophia and James had stopped before the shouting started?

What if one of them had said, "Let's pick together." or "You can choose tonight, and I'll pick next time."

The TV wouldn't still be paused. The dog wouldn't be barking. And no one would be sitting there red-faced and upset.

That's the thing about loud voices— they don't fix the problem; they make it harder to hear the solution.

Brave kids know how to press pause. Not the TV pause—the people pause. The one that gives you a moment to breathe, think, and speak kindly.

Different words can change everything.
"Let's take turns."
"We can figure this out."
"I'm sorry for yelling."

Those words turn the noise into peace. They help everyone feel safe enough to listen again.

Now it's your turn.
Think about a time when your voice got a little too loud— maybe with your brother or sister, or when a friend didn't listen. What could you have said instead?

That's how brave kids turn volume down—and kindness back up.

TEACHING FROM JESUS:

When voices get louder, it's hard to hear anyone— including Me. But when you soften your words, you make space for peace to come in. I gave you the power to bring calm into any room you walk into. You don't need to win the argument; you just need to bring the peace. That's what *real* strength looks like.

A gentle answer turns away wrath, but a harsh word stirs up anger."
— Proverbs 15:1

Words That Grow With You

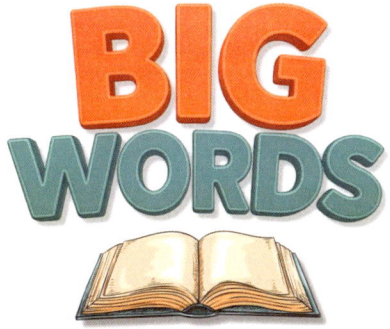

Flickered: *Flashed on and off quickly, like a light that's about to go out.*
The TV screen flickered while Sophia and James argued about whose turn it was.

Barked: *Spoke suddenly and sharply, like a quick shout.*
"No way!" James barked back, his voice louder than before.

Overlapped: *Happened at the same time, covering or blending over something else.*
Sophia's shouting overlapped James's, so neither could hear the other.

Fuming: *Feeling so angry that it's like steam is coming out of your ears.*
Both kids stood there fuming while the broken remote lay on the floor.

When you speak truth with love, hearts start to heal.

PART TWO

How to Choose Differently

Learning self-awareness and self-control; with courage and grace.

You've seen how arguments work. You've felt how they pull you in — louder, harder, stronger—until nobody really wins.

But now comes the brave part. This is where you learn how to **choose different**. Not because someone told you to. Not because you're afraid of getting in trouble. But because you can.

Choosing different doesn't mean being perfect. It means paying attention—to your words, your body, your feelings—and learning how to press **pause** before things get too loud.

In these next chapters, you'll learn how to:
- stay calm, even when your voice wants to shout.
- speak with courage, even when your heart feels shaky.
- and use words that bring people closer instead of pushing them away.

Because every choice you make shows the world who you are—not just what you do, but who you're becoming.

And every time you choose different...
you choose better.
You choose brave.
You choose YOU.

CHAPTER FOUR
The Lego Tower

Nathan had been working on his Lego tower for almost two hours. It wasn't just tall—it was detailed. Windows, doors, even a little flag at the top.

He leaned back and smiled. "At this rate, it might be taller than me," he thought proudly.

That's when his little sister, Opal, came zooming in. She was seven, holding her Barbie and purple convertible car.

"Vroom, vroom!" she shouted, pushing it across the floor.

Nathan's eyes went wide. "Careful!" he said sharply. But before you know it—

The Barbie car clipped the bottom row.

The tower shook, wobbled, and toppled into a pile of colorful pieces.

Nathan froze. His face burned hot.
His jaw clenched tight. He felt like
his whole body was a balloon ready
to burst.

"You ruined it!" he shouted, fists
tight at his sides.

Opal gasped. Her eyes watered.
"I didn't mean to," she whispered,
clutching her Barbie close.

But Nathan could barely hear her.
His thoughts roared louder than her voice: She always messes
things up. She doesn't even care how hard I worked. It was like
something boiling inside him— louder, hotter, bubbling up— ready
to spill over.

He wanted to scream. He wanted to stomp. He wanted to make
her feel how he felt— angry, small and out of control. But deep
down, another feeling stirred— a tiny one, quieter than the rest.

It sounded almost like a whisper, "Breathe."

Nathan's chest rose and fell. He could still feel
the heat in his face, the shake in his hands—
but the whisper stayed. "Breathe." He looked
down at the pieces scattered on the carpet.

The tower he had worked so hard on was gone.
But the pieces were still there—and so was Opal.

The Boiling Pot

When we're upset, our bodies try to tell us something.

Our hearts beat faster.
Our faces feel warm.
Our voices get louder.
Those are clues — not signs to yell — but signs to pause.

Nathan wasn't just mad because his tower fell. He had been working so hard on it and felt proud. Opal wasn't trying to ruin anything. She was excited to show him her new purple car. But neither of them stopped long enough to notice what was really going on inside. And when we ignore those clues, our feelings start to bubble — just like a pot of mac and cheese on the stove.

Imagine you're cooking. At first, the water is calm. Then bubbles start to rise — a few at a time, then faster. If you don't stir or turn the heat down, it boils over and spills everywhere.

That's what happens when we don't take care of the feelings building inside. They bubble up until they spill out in ways we don't mean — like yelling, stomping, or saying something we wish we hadn't.

Brave kids learn to notice the bubbles before they spill over. They turn the heat down. They take a breath.

They use brave words like:
"I'm feeling frustrated."
"I need a minute."

That's what it means to control yourself — not to hide your feelings, but to handle them with calm and courage.

BRAVE WORDS IN ACTION

What if Nathan had paused when he felt that first bubble of frustration rise up?
What if Opal had slowed down her purple convertible before zooming in so fast? What if she had stopped long enough to notice that Nathan was building something important?

Maybe the tower wouldn't have toppled. Maybe Nathan wouldn't have shouted. That's the thing about feelings— they don't stay quiet forever. If we ignore them, they bubble up and spill over, just like that pot on the stove.

But when we pay attention, we can turn the heat down before it boils. Brave kids don't let their feelings boss them around.
They pause.
They notice what's happening inside.

And they choose calmer words that help instead of hurt. Like:
"I'm feeling frustrated."
"I need a minute."
"Can we try again?"

Those words don't just stop an argument— they protect peace.

Now say this out loud:
"I can slow down before I boil over."

That's what brave kids do. They learn to notice the bubbles— and choose calm before it spills out.

I need a minute.

TEACHING FROM JESUS:

Sometimes your heart can feel like a pot that's ready to boil over. When that happens, step back and breathe. I can calm what feels too hot to handle. Listening first gives love time to grow—and that's what turns anger into understanding. *You don't have to win the moment; you can choose peace instead.*

Everyone should be quick to listen, slow to speak
and slow to become angry."
— James 1:19

Words That Grow With You

Detailed: *Full of small parts or tiny designs that make something special.*
Nathan's Lego tower was so detailed it even had a tiny door and a roof with patterns.

Clipped: *To bump or hit something lightly, just enough to make it move or fall.*
Opal's Barbie car clipped the edge of Nathan's tower, and the blocks started to wobble.

Boiling: *Getting hotter and hotter — like water bubbling in a pot.*
Nathan's frustration was boiling inside, ready to spill over like pot on the stove.

Crumbled: *Fell apart into little pieces.*
The Lego tower crumbled to the floor as both kids froze in surprise.

You don't lose anything by saying sorry—you gain connection.

CHAPTER FIVE
Spilled Tea

The kitchen was warm and smelled like dinner — roasted chicken and garlic bread. The sound of clinking dishes and soft music made the house feel cozy. Emma loved helping her dad set the table. It made her feel grown up.

Her dad smiled from the stove. "Can you pour the tea, sweetheart?"

She nodded proudly. The big glass pitcher was heavy, filled all the way to the top. She wrapped her hands around it, feeling the cool glass press against her palms.

I've got this, she told herself. She leaned over the table, trying to pour slowly, but her fingers wobbled under the weight.

The tea tilted — then suddenly

Sweet tea rushed across the table, spilling over napkins, dripping onto the floor, splattering her socks.

Emma froze. Her stomach twisted into a knot. Her heart raced. "Oh no," she whispered.

Her dad turned sharply, eyes wide. "Emma!" His voice cracked through the kitchen.

Her chest tightened. "I'm sorry! I didn't mean to!"

The silence that followed felt heavy — like the air had stopped moving. Her dad sighed, staring at the sticky puddle. His shoulders dropped.

Emma's eyes filled with tears. She waited for him to yell. Instead, he took a deep, quiet breath and walked over to her.

He grabbed a towel and handed her one, too. "Let's pause," he said softly. "It's just tea."

They knelt beside each other, wiping up the mess. The floor was sticky, their socks were wet, and the pitcher sat half empty — but the room began to calm.

Emma whispered, "I really was just trying to help."
Her dad smiled a little. "I know. And I should've seen that before I snapped."

They both laughed quietly — a small laugh, but a real one. Dinner went on. The chicken was warm, the bread buttery, the table clean again.

But Emma learned something bigger than how to pour tea. She learned how different things feel when you pause instead of letting your frustration take over.

The PAUSE Button

Sometimes life feels like it's about to spill over — like that tea.
One little thing goes wrong, and suddenly, it feels like
everything's gone wrong.

That's when you need your **pause** button.

Think about your favorite video game. When things get too wild
or you're about to lose, what do you do?

You press **pause**.

The game freezes. You breathe. You reset.
That's what it means to control the moment.

Pausing doesn't mean ignoring what happened. It means you give
yourself a second to think — so your feelings don't spill
everywhere.

Brave kids use brave words like:
"I can **pause** before I yell."
"I can take a breath before I speak."
"I can fix it without freaking out."

Because when you pause, you make space for calm — and that's
where better choices live.

BRAVE WORDS IN ACTION

What if Emma's dad continued to yell at Emma?

What if she had slammed the pitcher down and run off crying?

Dinner would've turned cold. Both would've felt hurt. All over one accident.

But one pause — one quiet moment — turned it around.

That's the power of calm.
It doesn't fix the spill.
It fixes the connection.

Now think about your own
"spilled tea moment." Maybe it
wasn't tea — maybe it was a broken
toy, a forgotten paper, or a harsh word.

How did you react? Did you boil over or
pause? Let's practice: Take a deep breath.
In through your nose...Out through your mouth.

Now say out loud:
"I can pause before I react."

That's what brave kids do. They don't let spills decide their day.
They pause — clean it up — and choose calm.

TEACHING FROM JESUS:

When someone makes a mistake, remember—everyone spills sometimes. You can clean up messes with kindness instead of blame. The way you respond shows others how love looks in real life. Be gentle, offer help, and show the kind of grace you'd want if the cup was yours.

Do to others as you would have them do to you."
— Luke 6:31

Words That Grow With You

Wobbled: *Shook or moved back and forth when trying to stay steady.*
Emma's hands wobbled as she tried to pour the tea without spilling.

Twisted: *Turned or knotted tightly.*
Emma's stomach twisted into a knot when the tea splashed across the table.

Sighed: *Let out a deep breath to show sadness, relief, or tiredness.*
Her dad sighed, looking at the puddle of tea before grabbing a towel.

Frustration: *The feeling you get when something doesn't go the way you hoped.*
Emma learned what happens when you pause instead of pouring out your frustration.

Your words can calm a room faster than your voice can fill it.

CHAPTER SIX

The Math Problem

The kitchen was quiet except for the scratch of a pencil and the hum of the refrigerator. Caleb sat at the table, his math worksheet spread out in front of him.

He had finished the first few problems just fine. But then came the word problems—the ones that made numbers sound like puzzles.

He read the same line three times. "Ben has 42 apples..." His eyes blurred. His hand tightened around the pencil.

"Mom," he groaned, "I don't get it."

She looked up from washing dishes. "Which part, buddy?"

"All of it!" Caleb snapped. His voice rose without meaning to. "It doesn't make sense!"

He pressed his palms against his forehead. His shoulders curled forward. Inside, it felt like a storm was building—fast.

His heartbeat pounded in his ears.
His face burned.
His chest felt tight.

"Take a breath," Mom said softly, drying her hands. "I can't!" he shouted. "It's too hard!"

She crouched next to him and spoke quietly. "Hey, Caleb... your storm's showing." He blinked. "What?"

Your body," she said gently. "It's giving me storm clues. Look at your hands—they're tight. Your breath is fast. That means your brain needs a break before you can think clearly again."

Caleb crossed his arms, still frowning. But his eyes started to soften. Mom didn't scold him. She just said, "Let's go get a drink of water and walk to the porch for a minute."

At first, Caleb didn't want to move. But as soon as he stepped outside, the cool air touched his skin. He took one slow breath. Then another. The thunder in his chest softened.

After a few quiet minutes, Mom asked, "What do you think your body was trying to tell you back there?"

He thought for a second. "That I was tired, maybe even a little hungry. And... frustrated."

She nodded. "That makes sense. You'd worked hard all day. Sometimes our brains yell when they really just need rest."

They went back inside. Caleb picked up his pencil again. The problem hadn't changed—but he had. This time, his brain was calm enough to think

He finished the worksheet. When he showed his mom, she smiled. "Looks like the storm has passed."

Caleb grinned. "Next time I'll catch it before it gets that big."

Body Clues

Your body always gives clues before your words do. A fast heartbeat, tight fists, hot cheeks, or shaky hands— they're like lightning flashes before the thunder.

Those clues don't mean something is wrong — they just mean a storm is starting to build inside.

And brave kids don't ignore the clues.
They notice them.
They pause.
They breathe.

When you slow down your body, you calm your brain, and your heart follows.

"I can feel my storm."
"I can slow it down."
"I can choose calm before I choose words."

Because controlling the pace isn't about being perfect.
It's about noticing what's happening inside you before the storm takes over.

BRAVE WORDS IN ACTION

What if Caleb had stayed in the storm?
He might've yelled, thrown his pencil, and stomped away.
His homework would still be there—unfinished—and his feelings
would still be heavy.

But instead, he slowed down, took a breath, and started again.
Because when you calm your storm, you calm the space around
you too.

Now it's your turn:
Think of the last time you felt a storm inside you.

What did your body do first?
Your hands? Your face? Your chest?

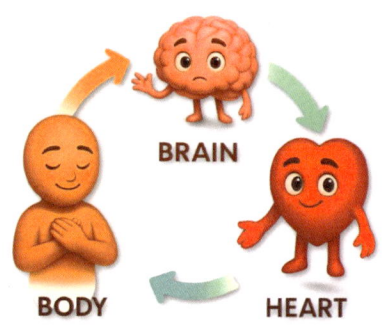

Next time, when you notice those clues, say quietly to yourself:
"This is just my storm talking. I can slow it down."

Practice taking three calm breaths.
One for your body.
One for your brain.
One for your heart.

That's how brave kids control the pace.

TEACHING FROM JESUS:

When your body feels tense and your thoughts swirl like thunderclouds, you can still find calm. My peace is already inside you; you just have to slow down and notice it. Take a deep breath and remember—I'm with you, even in the storm. When you rest in Me, your heart quiets too.

Peace I leave with you; my peace I give you.
— John 14:27

Words That Grow With You

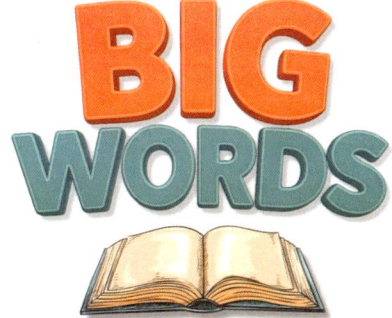

Blurred: *When something becomes fuzzy or unclear to your eyes—like it's hard to see clearly.*
Caleb's eyes blurred after reading the same line three times.

Groaned: *A low sound made when you're frustrated, tired, or upset.*
"Mom," Caleb groaned, "I don't get it."

Tightened: *To squeeze or hold something harder, often when you're tense or upset.*
His hand tightened around the pencil as his frustration grew.

Frowning: *Pulling your eyebrows together and lips down when something is hard or upsetting.*
Caleb crossed his arms, still frowning as he tried to calm his storm.

When you protect someone's heart, you show what love looks like

PART THREE
Speak With Confidence
Finding your voice, setting boundaries, and standing tall with truth and kindness.

Your words are powerful.
They can tear down or build up.
They can close doors or open them.
But here's something most people—kids and adults—don't always realize:

Confidence isn't about being the loudest in the room.
It's not about shouting until people listen.
And it's never about being mean or a bully.
Real confidence shows up as being assertive.

That means standing in your truth, speaking clearly, and respecting yourself and others at the same time.

Confidence isn't a feeling you wait for—it's a choice you make. It shows up in how you use your voice: softly, boldly, and courageously—with respect and truth.

In these next chapters, you'll learn how to:
- Use your voice with courage, boldness, and truth.
- Say "no" with kindness—and mean it.
- Handle people who make things hard sometimes.

Brave kids don't just speak fast—they respond with calm, kindness, and courage.

They lead with truth, and they lead with their voice.

CHAPTER SEVEN
Our Inner Voice

Eric stared at the words on his paper. His project was good, he knew that. He had worked hard on it, writing out every sentence, making sure it said exactly what he wanted.

But now, sitting in class with twenty pairs of eyes around him, his hands shook just a little. His throat felt dry. And in his mind, the thoughts began to swirl:

What if I mess up?
What if I stutter?
What if they laugh?
What if I sound dumb?

Each thought stacked on top of the other, building a mountain in his mind. The more he listened, the bigger it grew.

That's when another voice—quieter, but stronger—spoke up. Hey, it's okay. You worked hard for this. You can do it. It was his Big Me, the part of him that believed the truth.

But Little Me—the worried part—was still afraid. Little Me whispered, Stay quiet. Stay safe.

Eric took a breath and decided to listen to Big Me instead. When the teacher finally called on him, he stood up. His voice trembled at first. "My story is called... A Place in Time."

His heart was pounding, but the more he read, the steadier he became. He looked up and saw his classmates leaning in, listening. Nobody laughed. Nobody rolled their eyes. The class was interested.

43

And that's when Eric realized something important:
It wasn't about being perfect. It wasn't about worrying what everyone else thought. It was about choosing which voice to believe— and being brave enough to speak from the one that told the truth.

He smiled and thought,
What if I had told myself a different story?
What if I had said, "What if I do great?"
What if everyone loves it?"

Because sometimes, the bravest words you'll ever say
are the ones you speak to yourself first.

Down the hall, in another classroom, someone else was fighting that same storm inside. Different faces, different fears—but the same quiet battle inside: that small voice that whispers, "What if I'm wrong?"

Now, in a third-grade classroom, Moriah stared at the math problem on the board.

Her teacher asked, "Who wants to try?"
Her hand slowly went up, but she yanked it back down. Her cheeks grew warm.

Her thoughts started racing:
What if I look silly?
What if I get it wrong?
What if everyone laughs?

Her stomach felt tight, and she curled her toes in her shoes. The teacher's voice was gentle: "Moriah, would you like to give it a try?"

Moriah's heart pounded. She wanted to say no. She wanted to stay quiet. But her feet moved anyway. She walked slowly to the board, holding the marker like it was heavier than it really was.

"It's... twelve," she whispered. For a moment, silence.

Then her teacher nodded. "Yes, Moriah. That's right."

Her classmates didn't laugh. No one rolled their eyes. In fact, a few kids even smiled.

Moriah blinked. That's it? she thought. I was so sure it would be a disaster.

Moriah learned that confidence starts with which voice you listen to. Little Me whispers, "What if I mess up?" Big Me answers, "It's okay to try." And the story she told herself began to change.

Moriah smiled as she sat back down. Because now she knew: confidence starts with the voice she chooses to believe.

Confidence Isn't Loud

Sometimes the loudest storm isn't around us — it's inside us.

It sounds like:
What if I mess up?
What if they laugh?
What if they think I'm weird?

When those thoughts start to swirl, we have to
pause and ask ourselves: Is this true?

Where is this thought coming from—truth,
or something I made up in my head?

Because inside each of us, there are two voices.
There's Big Me—the part that's calm, brave, and steady.
The one that says, "You've got this. Take a breath. Try again."

And then there's Little Me—the part that feels scared or unsure.
The one that says, "What if I mess up?" or "What if they don't
like me?"

Now, this is important to remember: Little Me isn't bad or
broken. Little Me's job is to keep you safe—maybe from
something that hurt before. But sometimes, Little Me tries so
hard to protect you that it ends up holding you back. It says,
"Don't try. Don't speak. Don't move."—because it thinks that
staying small will keep you safe.

That's when Big Me has to step in. Big Me can listen kindly and
still choose courage. Big Me says, "I know you're scared, but we
can do this. We're okay."

That's what real confidence sounds like. It's not loud. It's honest.

46

Confidence isn't about showing off or being the best. It's about remembering what's true when your thoughts start to build up—like stacking bricks in your mind.

If those bricks are built on fear, the wall wobbles. But if they're built on truth—on what God says about you—they stand strong. Because your brain listens to the words you tell it.

It builds stories out of them. If you say, "I can't do it," your brain believes you and starts closing doors.

But if you say, "I can try," or "I'm learning," or "God is with me," your brain starts building something better.

Every time you choose truth over fear, you strengthen Big Me. And every time you remind Little Me that you're safe, you grow a quiet kind of courage—the kind that lasts.

Because confidence doesn't come from being perfect. It comes from being honest, grounded, and brave enough to believe what's true.. even when it's hard.

BRAVE WORDS IN ACTION

You have two voices inside you. Big Me and Little Me. The one you listen to most is the one that grows. It's like planting seeds in your mind. Whatever you plant will grow stronger.

If you plant words like:
"I can't do this."
"I'll mess up."
"They'll laugh at me."

You'll grow worry and fear. Those thoughts spread fast like weeds in a garden.

But if you plant words like:
"I can try."
"I'll do my best."
"My voice matters."

You'll grow courage. You'll grow peace. You'll grow confidence.

The words you tell yourself are seeds planted in your heart and God helps them grow into what's meant for you next.

Take a look inside your thoughts today. If you find weeds of worry or fear, don't be hard on yourself—just pull them out, and plant something good in their place.

Say out loud:
"I can choose brave words."
"I can grow something better."

Each time you do, you grow something strong— a story filled with calm, courage, and truth.

TEACHING FROM JESUS:

Being brave doesn't mean you never feel nervous—it means you choose courage even when your hands shake. I'm right beside you when you speak, helping your voice stay steady. When you tell the truth and share your heart, you're showing the world My light. Remember, confidence doesn't come from being perfect—it comes from knowing you're never alone.

Be strong and courageous. Do not be afraid; do not be discouraged,
for the Lord your God will be with you wherever you go.
— Joshua 1:9

Words That Grow With You

Courageous: *Choosing to do something even when it feels scary.*
Eric realized being courageous wasn't about being perfect—it was about speaking up even when his hands shook.

Whispered: *To speak very softly, using little or no voice.*
Moriah whispered, "It's... twelve," her heart pounding in her chest.

Confidence: *Believing in yourself and your ability to try, even when you're nervous.*
Moriah learned that confidence starts with the story you tell yourself.

Doubt: *The feeling of not believing in yourself or being unsure.*
The small voice inside Eric's mind whispered doubt—"What if I'm not enough?"—until he chose to believe something truer.

Teamwork grows stronger when we care more about each other than being first.

CHAPTER EIGHT
The Rainbow Markers

The classroom buzzed with chatter and the scratch of crayons.
Layla sat at her desk, grinning at the brand-new box of markers
she'd brought from home.

They were lined up in perfect rainbow order — red to violet —
every cap clicked tight. Her favorite was the sky blue.

"Okay, everyone," said Ms. Diaz. "You can start your art projects!"

Layla opened the box carefully, like a treasure chest.
But before she could draw her first line, a classmate leaned over.

"Whoa, those are so cool!
Can I use them?"

Layla froze. She liked
sharing… but these were her
special markers. She
pictured the smashed tips,
the lost caps, the rainbow all
mixed up. Her stomach did a little flip.

She didn't want to sound mean. If I say no, she thought, he'll think
I'm selfish. So she mumbled, "Uh… sure," and slid the whole box
across the table.

By the end of class, the rainbow was gone.
Caps were loose, a few colors had rolled under the desk, and the
blue marker tip was squished flat.

Layla's chest sank. The drawing didn't feel fun anymore.

That night, she told her mom, "I let everyone use my markers...
and now they're ruined." Her mom smiled gently. "What could you
have done differently," she asked, "now that you know how you
feel?"

Layla thought for a second. "Well, if I knew they were going to
get ruined, I wouldn't have shared them."

Her mom nodded. "That makes sense. But what if you knew they
wouldn't get ruined — would you still have wanted to share?"
Layla hesitated, then shook her head. "Maybe not. They're special
to me."

Her mom smiled. "See? You can be
kind and still take care of what's
yours. That's not being mean — that's
being wise and choosing wisely."

The next week, when art time
came again, the same classmate
reached over. "Can I use your
markers?"

Layla took a deep breath. "Not this time,"
she said. Her voice was calm, steady,
and sure. The classmate blinked,
then smiled. "Okay!"

Layla smiled back. The rainbow
stayed bright, and so did her heart. She realized something
powerful: You don't have to say "yes" to everyone to be kind.
Sometimes, kindness means protecting what matters to you.

The Invisible Fence

Boundaries are like invisible fences. They show people where "yes" ends and "no" begins.

Think about the fence around a playground. The fence doesn't stop kids from running, climbing, or playing tag. It's not there to ruin the fun — it's there to keep everyone safe inside.

Boundaries in friendships and family work the same way. They don't stop the fun or the love. They actually protect it.

Layla learned this with her markers. Her boundary wasn't about being mean — it was about being clear.

When she said "not this time," she wasn't shutting her friend out. She was keeping her rainbow safe — and that's okay.

Brave words don't always sound loud. Sometimes they sound calm and kind, like:

"Not this time."
"I want to keep this one special."
"You can use a few, but I want to save the rest."

Setting a boundary doesn't make you selfish. It shows that you respect yourself and others.

Because when you take care of what matters to you, you have more love, time, and energy to share later.

BRAVE WORDS IN ACTION

When Layla said yes the first time, she wasn't being "bad." She just didn't want to disappoint anyone.

But saying yes when you really mean no doesn't make things easier — it just makes your heart feel heavy later. The next time she said, "Not this time," something different happened. Her markers stayed safe. Her heart stayed calm. And her friendship stayed strong.

That's the power of brave words. They don't push people away — they teach others how to treat you with care.

Pause and think:
Is there something you've said "yes" to when you really wanted to say "no"? Maybe someone wanted to borrow your favorite toy. Or pick a game you didn't want to play. Or talk when you needed quiet time.

You can still be kind and say what you need.

Try saying these out loud:
"I need a little space right now."
"That's mine, and I'm not ready to share it yet."
"I like that idea, but can we do it a different way?"

TEACHING FROM JESUS:

Saying "no" can feel hard, but it's a brave way to protect what matters to you. You can be kind and firm at the same time. When you speak clearly and honestly, people learn how to respect your space. Boundaries aren't walls—they're gentle fences that help love stay safe and strong.

Let your 'Yes' be 'Yes,' and your 'No,' be 'No.'
— Matthew 5:37

Words That Grow With You

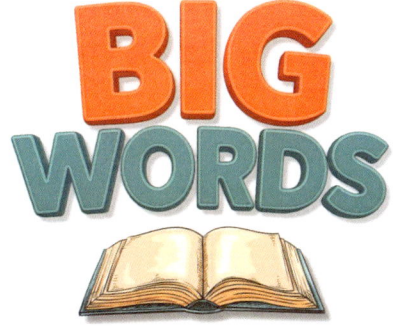

Treasure: *Something very special that you care about deeply.*
Layla opened the box carefully, like a treasure chest filled with magic colors.

Hesitated: *To stop or pause for a moment because you're unsure*
Layla hesitated before saying no, afraid her friend might think she was being unkind.

Wise: *Showing good judgment or making choices that protect what's important.*
Her mom smiled and said, "That's not being mean—that's being wise and choosing kindly."

Protect: *To keep something or someone safe from harm or damage.*
Layla learned that setting a boundary wasn't selfish—it helped protect what mattered to her.

Honesty brings freedom to your heart and light to the moment.

CHAPTER NINE
The Pushy Classmate

Maggie lined up at recess, ready for the swings. It was her favorite part of the playground — the place she could think, breathe, and feel free. The line was long, but she didn't mind waiting.

Behind her, Logan stomped up. "Hurry up," he muttered.
Maggie glanced back. "I'm waiting my turn."

Logan rolled his eyes. "Just move. I'll go first." He shoved his foot forward, trying to squeeze in front of her.
Maggie's chest tightened. Her fists balled at her sides. This isn't fair. Why does he always do this?

She thought about yelling, but her voice caught in her throat.
She thought about stepping aside, but her stomach twisted.
If I move, he'll keep doing it.

The swing squeaked as the first kid jumped off.
Now it was Maggie's turn. But Logan leaned forward again. "I said I'm next!"

Maggie's heart thumped in her chest. Her face felt hot, but she took a slow breath. Her voice shook a little — but she stood tall.

"No, Logan," she said. "It's my turn. You can go after me."

For a moment, Logan froze. Then he huffed and stepped back, kicking at the dirt.

Maggie climbed into the swing, her chest rising with relief.
The chains jingled as she pumped her legs, higher and higher.

She didn't yell.
She didn't shove.
She simply stood firm.

When the bell rang and the
kids ran back to class,
Mrs. Dempsey walked
beside her. I saw what
happened," she said quietly.

Maggie's stomach dropped.
"Am I in trouble?"

Mrs. Dempsey smiled. "No, you handled that with courage and
calm. You were firm with your words, but you said them with
kindness. That's what standing tall looks like."

Maggie smiled softly.

She hadn't realized that real strength could sound gentle — and
still stand its ground.

Standing Firm Isn't Mean

Sometimes people push — not just in line, but in life.
They push to get their way.
They push because they want control.
They push because they don't know how to use their words yet.

But when someone pushes you, it doesn't always mean you have to push back. It means you get to practice strength on the inside.

Think of a tree in the wind. When the wind blows hard, the tree doesn't shout or shove back. It bends a little. It stays rooted. It stands tall. That's real strength — steady, calm, and grounded.

Standing tall doesn't always look loud.
Sometimes it sounds calm.
Sometimes it sounds steady.

Sometimes it sounds like,
"No, that's not okay."
"It's my turn."
"Please don't do that."

Brave kids learn that **calm doesn't mean weak — it means wise.** And kindness doesn't mean giving in — it means knowing your worth, while still respecting others.

Because when you stand tall and stay kind, you show others what real confidence sounds like — just like that tree that never forgets its roots, even in the wind.

BRAVE WORDS IN ACTION

Words are a lot like roots. They grow deep — and they shape what happens next.

If you use angry words, the ground around you shakes. If you use calm words, the ground steadies again. That's why your words matter — they build the world you stand in.

When someone pushes — I want you to pause before you speak. Take a breath, like that tree in the wind.

Ask yourself,
"What kind of roots do I want to grow right now?"

Because every time you choose calm over yelling, kindness over giving in, and truth over silence — you grow stronger roots inside you. So next time someone pushes too hard, remember you don't have to shove back to stand tall. You just have to stay rooted in who you are.

Now, think about a time someone pushed past your boundaries — maybe they took your spot, grabbed what was yours, or talked over you when you were speaking.

What could you say next time that keeps your calm and your courage?
Try it out loud:
"It's still my turn right now."
"Please don't push me. I can wait my turn, and so can you."
"I'm not being mean, I'm just being clear."

Because brave kids don't have to be the loudest in the room — they just have to stay rooted in truth, calm, and kindness.

60

TEACHING FROM JESUS:

Standing tall isn't about being the loudest—it's about being steady in truth and gentle in spirit. When you speak with both courage and kindness, you reflect My heart. Love can be firm without being harsh. Every time you choose calm over chaos, you show others what real strength looks like.

Be on your guard; stand firm in the faith; be courageous; be strong.
Do everything in love.
— 1 Corinthians 16:13–14

Words That Grow With You

Firm: *Strong and steady — not easily moved or changed.*
Maggie's voice was calm but firm when she said, "It's my turn. You can go after me."

Grounded: *Feeling steady, calm, and sure of yourself.*
Standing grounded helped Maggie stay kind and confident, even when Logan pushed.

Relief: *The light, calm feeling that comes after something hard.*
When Maggie climbed onto the swing, her chest filled with relief.

Confidence: *The quiet strength that comes from believing in yourself and knowing your worth.*
Maggie realized that confidence doesn't have to shout — sometimes it sounds like calm.

A kind word can be the bridge back to belonging.

PART FOUR

Words That Connect

Restoring trust, repairing relationships, and building bridges through honesty.

Your words can build bridges or walls.
They can pull people closer or push them away.

This part of the book is about connection—
  · Seeing from another point of view.
  · Calming down when you feel defensive.
  · Having brave conversations that build understanding.

Brave kids don't just win arguments—

They build friendships stronger.
They listen as much as they speak.
And they use their voices to connect, not compete.

Because connection isn't about being right—it's about choosing kindness, even when it's hard.

Brave kids choose to build **bridges, not walls**.
That's how love stays strong.

CHAPTER TEN
A Different View

Aiden and Riley sat side by side at the same lab table during science time. The classroom lights glowed softly overhead, and each pair of students had a small tray with leaves, magnifying glasses, and color pencils. They were supposed to describe what color the leaf looked like under the light.

"It's dark green," Aiden said confidently, already writing it down on his worksheet.

Riley squinted at the same leaf. "No, it's light green—almost yellow, actually. You're not looking close enough." Aiden frowned and leaned in.

"I am looking. It's dark green. See?" Riley crossed her arms. "You're just saying that because you want to be right."

The room filled with quiet chatter and the faint sound of pencils scratching paper. But at their table, voices were rising.

"Maybe your eyes are tricking you," Aiden said, a little sharper this time. "Maybe your eyes are playing tricks on you!" Riley shot back, her cheeks getting pink.

It wasn't really about the leaf anymore. It was about who was right. The words started to pile up, one on top of another, like blocks about to topple. It felt heavy between them. Just then, Ms. Alvarez walked over. She didn't scold or sigh. She just gave a small smile, the kind that said she'd seen this before.

"She reached into the science bin and pulled out two pairs of sunglasses—the ones with different tinted lenses the class had used last week to learn about how color changes under light.

Try these," she said calmly. "Aiden, you take the black-tinted ones. Riley, you take the yellow." They slipped them on. Riley gasped. "Whoa! The leaf looks brown now!" Aiden blinked. "Wait—mine looks kind of black!"

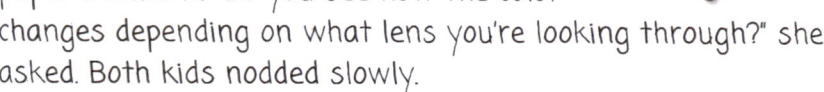

The two looked at each other, surprised. Then Ms. Alvarez placed the leaf under a small lamp and held up a white sheet of paper behind it. "Do you see how the color changes depending on what lens you're looking through?" she asked. Both kids nodded slowly.

"Neither of you were wrong," she said softly. "You were just seeing the same thing in a different way." Aiden stared down at the leaf. "So it's not really about who's right..." Riley finished his thought. "It's about what we're each seeing."

Ms. Alvarez smiled. "Exactly. Sometimes people see through different lenses. It doesn't mean their view is broken—it just means they're seeing from a different angle."

Aiden set the glasses down. "I guess next time, instead of arguing, we could... ask what the other person sees."

"Now, that's kindness," Ms. Alvarez said. "I'm proud of you both."

When the bell rang, Aiden and Riley packed up their papers. Before leaving, Riley grinned. "Hey, next time we have an argument, I'll remember to borrow your glasses."

Aiden laughed. "Deal."

Invisible Glasses

Sometimes we think everyone should see what we see. But the truth is—people wear different sunglasses. Not real ones. Invisible ones, made of their experiences, their feelings, and the way they were taught to look at the world.

That means two people can look at the same thing— a leaf, a problem, a friend— and see something completely different.

It doesn't always mean one of them is wrong. It just means they're seeing it through their own lens. When you understand that, everything changes.

You stop needing to be right all the time. You start wanting to understand. Brave kids don't just talk louder— they listen closer.

They ask questions like:
"What do you see that I don't?"
"Can you tell me how it looks from your side?"
"Maybe we're both right in different ways."

That's what real understanding sounds like. It's not about winning an argument. It's about trying on someone else's glasses for a moment—and seeing the situation the way they see it.

Take a slow breath. Think about someone you disagreed with recently. If you could borrow their "sunglasses" for a minute, what might you notice that you didn't before?

Because brave words don't say, "I'm right." They say, "I'm listening."

BRAVE WORDS IN ACTION

When Aiden and Riley stopped arguing, the leaf didn't change color—their words did. At first, they both wanted to be right. But being right didn't feel right anymore. Even if one of them "won," the space between them still felt heavy.

That's what happens when we use words to win instead of to connect. Harsh words stack up like blocks, turning into a wall between us. But brave words don't stack walls— they build bridges. They help us reach each other again. Brave kids choose the words that make connection possible.

Instead of saying, "You're wrong," they say, "That's interesting— what do you see?"
Instead of shouting, "That's not how it is!" they ask, "Can you tell me what makes you think that?"

Because brave kids know listening doesn't erase their own view it just adds more color to the picture. Now pause for a moment. Picture you and a friend arguing about something small—a game rule, a color, or who gets the first turn.

Can you imagine both of you wearing different sunglasses? Yours might be red. Theirs might be blue. You're both looking at the same thing—just through different lenses. Take a slow breath and ask yourself: "What might it look like through their glasses?"

Now say this out loud:
"I can listen before I speak."
"I can look through their lens."
"I can find the middle."

That's what brave communication sounds like—calm, kind, and the kind of listening that makes the world a little brighter.

TEACHING FROM JESUS:

You won't always see things the same way as someone else —and that's okay. I made each of you to notice the world differently. When you choose to listen instead of argue, you make space for friendship to grow. Curiosity builds bridges, not walls. You don't have to agree on everything to stay kind.

How good and pleasant it is when God's people live together in unity.
— Psalm 133:1

Words That Grow With You

Perspective: *The way someone sees or understands something, based on their own thoughts, feelings, and experiences.*
Aiden and Riley realized they weren't wrong—they just had different perspectives.

Argument: *When two or more people disagree and try to prove they're right.*
Their voices grew louder as the argument became more about being right than understanding.

Observation: *Something you notice or discover.*
The two of them wrote, "Observation: Green leaf. Conclusion: People see things differently."

Understanding: *Seeing a situation from another person's point of view and showing care instead of judgment.*
When Aiden listened, he found understanding was brighter than being right.

When you keep your word, others learn they can trust your heart.

CHAPTER ELEVEN
The Shield Goes Up

Hannah sat at her desk, tapping her pencil. The math worksheet in front of her was only half-finished, but she was racing through the problems anyway.

Her mind wasn't on math—it was on art class, her favorite part of the day. If I just finish fast, I'll have more time for painting, she told herself.

Her teacher, Mrs. Dawson, walked past, checking papers as she moved between desks. She paused beside Hannah's. "Hannah, are you rushing?" she asked gently. "Let's take some time to slow down and make sure your work is correct."

The words only annoyed Hannah more. Her cheeks warmed. The frustration bubbled up like a shaken soda can.

Why is she always checking on me? Hannah thought. I'm fine! Before she could stop herself, she muttered under her breath, "I'm not rushing." Her tone was sharp.

A couple of kids at the next table looked up. Hannah's stomach flipped. She ducked her head, pretending to stay focused, but her pencil moved faster.

She glanced around the room. Some kids were only halfway done, carefully checking each problem. Others were quietly erasing, double-checking their math. Nobody was racing the clock like she was. And that's when it hit her—deep down, she knew she had hurried.

But here's the truth: rushing didn't actually speed anything up.
Her answers were messy.
She'd skipped steps.
She'd probably have to go back and fix them anyway.

She sighed, realizing that hurrying hadn't saved her any time—it had only made more work for her later. The words she'd said—"I'm not rushing"—were like a little invisible shield.

It made her feel protected for a second, but it also blocked her from hearing her teacher's help. Mrs. Dawson hadn't been trying to scold her; she'd been trying to help her slow down.

Hannah took a deep breath.
She put down her pencil and reread her first few answers.
They weren't terrible, but they weren't her best. That's when she caught herself thinking— Maybe brave isn't finishing first. Maybe brave is slowing down, even when I really want to be done.

This is where brave kids pause.
They ask themselves:
"Is rushing really getting me closer?"
"Or is it slowing me down in the long run?"

Hannah smiled a little. Then she carefully
fixed her next problem, one step at a time.
And when art class finally came, she
realized something surprising—

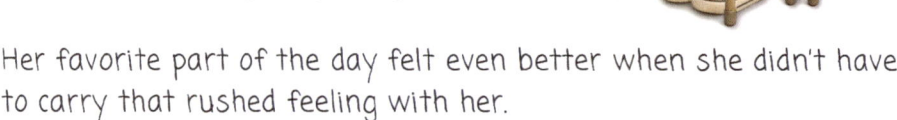

Her favorite part of the day felt even better when she didn't have to carry that rushed feeling with her.

The Closed Door

When someone points out something we could do better, it can make us feel uncomfortable, almost like we're in trouble.

We all have shields like that. Sometimes they sound like,
"I know!"
"I didn't!"
"You don't understand!"

We use them when we feel nervous or embarrassed. The shield makes us feel safe for a moment— but it also keeps us from hearing what could actually help us.

Think of it like this: When you close your bedroom door because you don't want anyone to bother you, it feels quiet and safe for a little while. But if someone was trying to help you find something you lost, they couldn't—because the door is closed. Defensiveness works the same way. It shuts people out right when they're trying to help us grow.

Because here's the truth: Feeling safe for a second isn't the same as noticing someone is actually trying to help. When Hannah finally lowered her shield, she realized her teacher wasn't trying to be mean— she was trying to help her slow down and do her best work.

That's what brave kids learn: When someone helps you notice something, it's not about being "in trouble." It's about being open to learn. Because sometimes the strongest thing you can do is open the door and let understanding walk in.

BRAVE WORDS IN ACTION

When Hannah said, "I'm not rushing," she wasn't trying to be rude — she was just trying to protect herself. That's what our "shields" do.

But what if she had said something different?
What if she had taken a deep breath and said, "I'll slow down." or "You're right, I was hurrying."

The whole moment would have changed. The shield would've lowered, and the sunshine could've peeked through.

Sometimes we think brave means fighting back. But brave also means being calm enough to listen. Strong enough to say, "You're right." And wise enough to pause before reacting.

Think about the last time you felt like putting your "shield" up— maybe when a teacher corrected you, or a parent reminded you to clean up, or a friend said you hurt their feelings.

Pause and ask yourself:
"Is my shield helping me learn?"
"Or is it blocking the light that could help me grow?"

Try using these brave words the next time it happens:
"Thanks for helping me."
"I didn't see it that way before."
"Can I try again?"

Every time you lower your shield, you let a little more light in. And that's how brave kids grow— not by being perfect, but by being teachable.

74

TEACHING FROM JESUS:

When someone helps you see where you can do better, it isn't to embarrass you—it's to help you grow. I know it's hard to hear correction, but that's how wisdom begins. Every time you listen with an open heart, you learn something new about who I've made you to be. Lower your shield, and let My light teach you.

Whoever loves discipline loves knowledge,
but whoever hates correction is foolish.
— Proverbs 12:1

Words That Grow With You

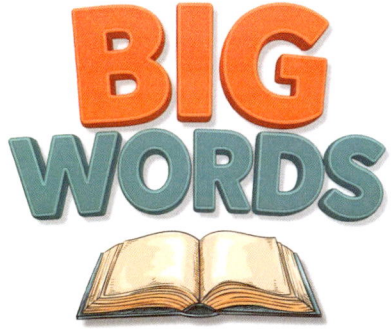

Defensive: *Acting like you need to protect yourself, even when no one is trying to hurt you.*
Hannah's voice sounded defensive when she said, "I'm not rushing!" because she felt embarrassed.

Frustration: *The feeling you get when something doesn't go the way you want, or when you feel misunderstood.*
Hannah's cheeks warmed with frustration as her teacher asked her to slow down.

Teachable: *Willing to listen, learn, and grow — even when something feels uncomfortable.*
When Hannah lowered her shield, she became teachable and started to see her teacher was trying to help.

Reflect: *To pause and think deeply about what happened and what you can learn from it.*
Brave kids reflect before reacting — they ask, "Is my shield helping me learn?"

You don't have to be perfect to shine—you just have to be real

CHAPTER TWELVE
The Squishy

Ella and Olivia had just finished dance class. Their hair was messy from practice, their shoes squeaked on the school hallway floors, and both of them laughed as they walked back toward their classrooms to grab their things.

Olivia always double-checked to make sure she didn't leave behind her water bottle or sweatshirt. But that day something caught her eye—a colorful box of squishies sitting on a desk in the classroom.

Her heart leapt. She spotted the one squishy she had really wanted. "No one's here," Olivia whispered to Ella. "The teacher already went home."

Olivia's fingers hovered over the box. Her cheeks grew warm. Before she could think twice, she grabbed the squishy. "You can take one too," she told Ella.

Both girls slipped out of the classroom, clutching their new prize. Later that afternoon, Olivia hopped into her mom's car after dance.

She held up the squishy with pride. "Look what I got!" Her mom smiled at first. "Oh wow! How did you earn that?"

The question stopped Olivia cold. Her face shifted. She couldn't hide the truth anymore. "I... I didn't earn it. I took it from the classroom." Her mom's smile faded into concern. "Olivia, do you think that was the right choice?"

Olivia's stomach sank. She shook her head. She knew it wasn't right, but inside she wrestled. What do I do now?

Her mom placed a hand on hers. "Sweetheart, this is hard, but this is also where brave conversations live. You have a choice: to cover it up and ignore it—or to choose differently."

So, Olivia decided. First, she went back into the classroom and quietly returned the squishy to the box. But even after putting it back, her stomach still didn't feel right.

That evening at home, she just couldn't shake the weight of what happened. It was like carrying that heavy backpack stuffed with rocks. She replayed the moment in her mind, wondering what her teacher would say if she found out.

By morning, Olivia knew what she needed to do.

Returning the squishy wasn't enough. She also had to tell the truth. She wanted her teacher to hear it from her—not from anyone else.

As she walked toward the classroom her legs felt wobbly, and thoughts started swirling through her head.

What if my teacher gets mad?
What if she never trusts me again?
What if she thinks I'm not a good student?

The story in her head felt bigger and scarier than the truth.

Finally, she stood before the teacher and softly said, "I took a squishy yesterday when you weren't here. I also told Ella she could have one too. I put it in my backpack and then realized I shouldn't have. I wanted to tell you the truth."

Her teacher looked surprised, but she knelt down and said, "Olivia, thank you for being honest. That was really brave. I forgive you. You've shown me I can trust you to tell the truth."

In that moment, Olivia felt the backpack of invisible bricks lift.

She realized something powerful:
Returning the squishy fixed the action.
But telling the truth repaired the trust.

Fixing vs. Repairing

Telling the truth can feel like standing on the edge of a really tall diving board. Your knees shake, your heart races, and every part of you wants to climb back down. That's how Olivia felt.

She had already returned the squishy—but her heart still felt heavy, like a backpack full of invisible bricks. Because sometimes, fixing what we did on the outside isn't the same as repairing what's going on inside our heart.

That's where the voice in our head starts to talk. Little Me might whisper,

"What if my teacher gets mad?"
"What if she never trusts me again?"
"What if everyone thinks I'm bad student?"

But Big Me knows something different. Big Me knows the truth doesn't make you a bad person— it helps you come back to peace.

So when Olivia took a breath and told the truth, it was like setting that heavy backpack down. Her heart felt lighter, **because she wasn't hiding anymore.**

That's what truth does—it opens the door for repair. It helps your heart catch up to your actions.

Brave words sound like this:
"I need to tell you something."
"I did it, and I want to make it right."
"I'm sorry, and I'm ready to fix it."

When you say brave words, you remind Little Me that you're safe now— that honesty is how we grow.

Because brave kids know this: Mistakes don't make you a bad. They make you human. And honesty helps your heart heal.

That's the kind of courage that builds trust— the kind that starts on the inside and shines through everything you do.

BRAVE WORDS IN ACTION

When Olivia first told herself, "It's fine—no one will know," she was really saying, "I don't want to feel this feeling." Which is completely understandable.

But when she finally spoke the truth, something different happened— the fear started to fade. Because hiding the truth is like trying to hold a beach ball underwater. You can press it down for a while, but it always finds a way to pop back up.

The truth has a way of rising— and when it does, peace rises with it.

When Olivia told the truth, her shoulders dropped, her chest felt lighter, and the feeling in her stomach went away.

That's what freedom feels like— not loud or flashy., but quiet and calm on the inside.

Now it's your turn to think: Is there something small you need to make right? A truth you've been afraid to say out loud? Or maybe a moment where honesty could fix a friendship?

Pause and remember:
Returning the squishy fixed the action.
But telling the truth repaired the trust.

And every time you choose honesty, your heart learns it's safe to tell the truth again. You don't have to be perfect to be brave. You just have to be honest— and honesty always lightens the load.

TEACHING FROM JESUS:

When you make a mistake, don't hide it—bring it into the light. Telling the truth shows that your heart wants to grow. I don't hold your wrong choices against you; I use them to teach you. *Honesty lifts the weight you're carrying and replaces it with peace.* That's what forgiveness feels like—freedom.

If we confess our sins, He is faithful and just to forgive us our sins and to cleanse us from all unrighteousness.
— 1 John 1:9

Words That Grow With You

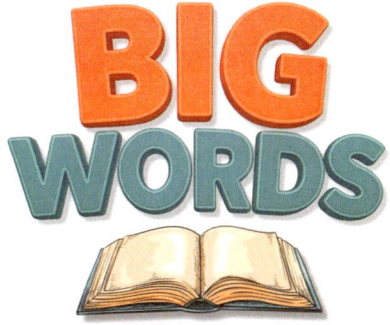

Clutching: *To hold something tightly or closely, especially when you don't want to let it go.*
Both girls slipped out of the classroom, clutching their new prize.

Concern: *A feeling of worry, care, or sympathy for someone or something.*
Her mom's smile faded into concern when she heard what Olivia had done.

Wrestled: *To struggle with a difficult thought, feeling, or decision.*
Olivia knew it wasn't right, but inside she wrestled— "What do I do now?"

Repaired: *To fix or make something right again.*
Returning the squishy fixed the action, but telling the truth repaired the trust.

he strongest words aren't loud—they're true, kind, and full of grace.

CLOSING

If you've made it here, it means you've practiced one of the bravest things any person can do—listening, learning, and choosing your words with care.

You've seen how words can build or break, how tone can open or close doors, and how sometimes the quietest moments hold the most courage. You've learned that being brave doesn't always mean being loud.

Sometimes it means pausing before reacting. Sometimes it means saying, "I'm sorry." And sometimes, it means standing firm in truth when it would be easier to stay silent.

You've discovered that words can change moments—and moments can change relationships. And maybe the most important truth of all:

Bravery grows in the small, everyday choices you make.

Each time you pause, listen, forgive, or speak truthfully, you make the world a little softer, a little kinder, and a little more connected.

So when you find yourself in a moment where you don't know what to say—pause. Breathe. Think back to what you've learned here. The brave words are still inside you, waiting to be spoken when the time comes.

You've become a *Brave Conversations Kid*.
And the world needs more people like you.

Now, take a deep breath—because what comes next matters just as much as everything you've learned:
a conversation from my heart to yours—the conversation that closes the gap.

The Conversation That Closes the Gap

I've spent a lot of time thinking about words—how they can build or break, heal or hurt, open or close. Sometimes we use them to protect ourselves. Sometimes we use them to reach for someone we love. And sometimes… we avoid using them at all.

Lately, I've noticed how easy it's become to go silent—especially when something feels uncomfortable, when someone sees the world differently than we do, or when deep down, we know we're the ones who need to make things right.

Silence feels safer in the moment.
But safety isn't the same as connection.

Here's what I've learned: **Conversation is one of the quietest—and bravest—acts of courage there is.** Staying in the room takes strength. Listening when your emotions want to run is a kind of maturity you don't outgrow. And listening doesn't mean agreeing—it simply means you care enough to understand.

We live in a world loud with opinions and quiet with understanding. People talk over each other, past each other, or not at all. When we stop listening, something subtle happens: we stop seeing the person behind the words. And once that happens, assumptions rush in to fill the silence.

Assumptions about motives.
Assumptions about beliefs.
Assumptions about someone's heart.

The longer we stay silent, the heavier those assumptions become—until we're not just misunderstanding each other… we're quietly drifting from each other.

And all of it could've been softened by one honest conversation.

But fear doesn't have to be our ending. Fear can be a signal —an invitation to lean in, not pull away. That's where curiosity comes in.

Curiosity is the bridge that brings us back. It's what happens when we trade judgment for wonder, defensiveness for questions, and silence for courage.

Curiosity sounds like:
   "That's new for me—can you tell me more?"
   "I see it differently—can I share my side?"
   "What made you feel that way?"

When we lead with curiosity, we're not trying to win. We're trying to understand. We remember that we can learn from anyone—even when we disagree.

Because sometimes the goal isn't to change someone's mind. It's to see their heart.

Not to excuse what's wrong, but to understand where it came from. Pain has a story. Fear has a beginning. Words have roots.

When you pause long enough to look beyond the comment, the tone, or the reaction, you'll usually find something tender underneath—something that deserves compassion, even if you don't agree.

And when you feel offended or frustrated by someone's words? You're not broken. You're human. And that feeling is not an insult—it's an invitation to understand what's happening inside you.

Ask yourself:
  "Why did that hit me that way?"
  "What is this bringing up in me?"
  "Is this about their words—or something deeper in me?"

Often, it's not the sentence that hurts—it's the memory, the wound, or the belief inside us that suddenly feels exposed. And when you look at that with honesty, you grow. You become more aware of yourself—and that makes room to understand others too.

That's how communication becomes more than words. It becomes a bridge—a connection point between what's real in you and what's real in someone else.

Communication is not about who's right. It's about who's willing to stay honest, stay kind, and stay open.

Connection doesn't require sameness. Connection requires respect. It means remembering that behind every opinion is a person. Behind every reaction is a story. Behind every belief is a reason.

When we stop communicating out of fear, we lose the chance to understand each other. But when we speak with kindness and listen with courage, something strong begins to grow—something walls can't stop and assumptions can't break: *connection.*

Because love isn't proven in winning the argument. Love is proven in staying present.

Real bravery isn't loud. It's steady. It's humble. It's __choosing__ to stay in the conversation when silence would be easier.

Every time you choose to speak honestly, listen fully, or ask a question instead of assuming—you make the world just a little more connected.

And someday, someone will need your voice. They'll need your calmness, your courage, your clarity, your willingness to stay in the room. They'll need to see that truth and love can live in the same sentence.

So don't be afraid to speak. Don't be afraid to listen. And don't be afraid to stay— even when the conversation feels big.

Because that's how we grow:
one *honest* word,
one *brave* moment,
one *conversation* at a time.

"Let your conversation be always full of grace, seasoned with salt, so that you may know how to answer everyone."
—Colossians 4:6

THE TUG
S E R I E S

The Journey Doesn't End Here
Tug of Words is just the beginning.

The Tug Series was created to help families grow in truth, courage, empathy, and emotional awareness—one conversation at a time. And there's more to come.

In the upcoming books, we'll explore deeper themes of the heart—how kids think, how they feel, how they communicate, and how they build confidence from the inside out. Each new release will help children understand themselves better and connect with others through compassion, courage, and biblical truth.

Stay tuned for what's next.
And grow with us.

Follow along for sneak peeks, updates, and tools for families, teachers, and coaches who want to raise kids who listen well, speak truthfully, and love deeply.

Because the conversations we start now can change a generation.

I AM A
BRAVE
CONVERSATIONS
KID

This certificate is awarded to

_____

for learning to speak with courage
and respect.

Signed _____

PARENT & TEACHER NOTES

Dear Parents, Teachers, and Mentors,

This book was written for children, but its truths reach far beyond childhood. Words are powerful—they can either wound or heal, divide or connect. Our goal with Tug of Words is to equip kids with tools they can use in everyday life—at home, at school, and with friends.

Here are some ways you can help bring the lessons to life:

- Model brave words. Let kids hear you use phrases like "I need space" or "Let's share." Children learn best by watching.
- Role-play. Practice the Brave Words sections out loud. Make it fun and silly—pretend you're on stage or in a game.
- Pause together. The "pause button" works for adults, too. When things get tense, try stopping together and taking a breath before speaking.
- Celebrate small wins. When your child chooses to handle conflict with kindness or courage, notice it. Praise the effort, not just the result.
- Revisit often. This book isn't meant to sit on a shelf. Pull it back out during tricky seasons—new school years, friendship struggles, or family transitions.

Most importantly: remind your child this isn't about being a "good kid." It's about becoming someone who takes ownership of their choices, builds connection, and speaks truth with love.

RACHEL CLOSSON

Rachel Closson is a Certified High-Performance Coach, International Speaker, devoted wife and mother, and the author of Tug of Words: Speak with Confidence and Truth.

At the time of writing this book, Rachel's two children were seven and fifteen—a season that inspired much of her heart behind Tug of Words.

Her lifelong walk with God has shaped every part of how she communicates, leads, and loves. It's where she's learned that real growth begins with humility, that strength and softness can coexist, and that listening —both to God and to others—is one of the holiest acts of love.

This faith-driven lens influences how Rachel parents, coaches, and writes: with honesty, discernment, and compassion. She believes that truth is not just something we speak, but something we live—in our tone, our choices, and our willingness to be transformed by God's refining hand.

Through her own journey of self-awareness and faith, Rachel discovered that helping her kids—and others—find their voice begins with anchoring truth in Him.

Rachel's deepest desire is that her children, and every child who reads this book, will have a heart that seeks Jesus— because that's where truth is found.

Through her coaching and writing, Rachel challenges women to take ownership of their healing—because your children don't become who you tell them to be; they become who you are. She teaches women and families to live with courage, truth, and grace, and to use words that build connection instead of break it.

She believes that words matter. They shape relationships, build trust, and reflect the authenticity God calls each of us to carry.

Rachel lives this message in her everyday life—whether sharing quiet mornings on the porch, tending her garden, collecting eggs from her chickens, or spending time with her husband, children, and parents.

To learn more about Rachel's work, coaching, and message of alignment through faith and truth, visit RachelClosson.com.

"YOU WILL KNOW THE TRUTH, AND THE TRUTH WILL SET YOU FREE."
— JOHN 8:32

EMPOWERMENT THROUGH *gratitude* JOURNAL

Continue your journey of reflection and faith through our Empowerment Through Gratitude Journals.

EMPOWERMENT THROUGH GRATITUDE PREK-3RD EDITION

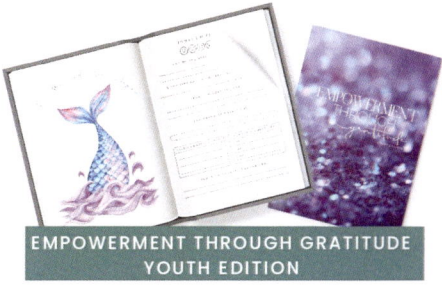

EMPOWERMENT THROUGH GRATITUDE YOUTH EDITION

EMPOWERMENT THROUGH GRATITUDE TEEN EDITION

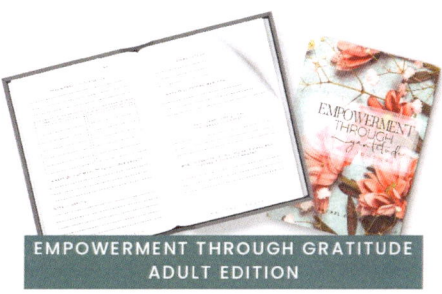

EMPOWERMENT THROUGH GRATITUDE ADULT EDITION

Available on Amazon